OKLAHOMA
CITY
ZOO
ENTRANCE

THE
GREAT
LEOPARD
HUNT

THE GREAT LEOPARD HUNT

WRITTEN & ILLUSTRATED
by CAROLYN MACY

Dedicated to my family and friends. Thank you OKC Zoo personnel, Amy Stevens and Candice Rennels, for helping me with my research.

Published by Tate Publishing & Enterprises, LLC
127 E. Trade Center Terrace | Mustang, Oklahoma 73064 USA
1.888.361.9473 | www.tatepublishing.com

Tate Publishing is committed to excellence in the publishing industry. The company reflects the philosophy established by the founders, based on Psalm 68:11,
"The Lord gave the word and great was the company of those who published it."

Book design copyright © 2015 by Carolyn Macy.
Written and Illustrated by Carolyn Macy

Published in the United States of America

ISBN: 978-1-68254-312-2
1. JUVENILE NONFICTION / Animals / Jungle Animals
2. JUVENILE NONFICTION / History / United States / Oklahoma
15.08.03

The jungle loomed dark and the jungle lay deep
With secrets it guarded and promised to keep,
From its canopied top to its deepest ravine,
By hiding its life in dense foliage of green.

Spied resting atop of a branch on a tree,
And drowsily watching all things he could see,
Lay a leopard in prime in his fine, spotted coat
With rumbling contentment escaping his throat.

The Fates had decreed that this leopard who lay,
Stretched out and enjoying the warmth of the day
In his India jungle, would journey abroad
To plains far away where the Indians trod.

One warm winter day as some winter days go,
This fine captured feline kept pacing below
While his eyes searched above for a place he could leap
To escape from this prison so rocky and deep.

His amber eyes narrowed ablaze with their glow.
Fierce anger welled up, and his throat rumbled low.
With a flick of his tail and brute muscle control,
His body released and took flight with his soul.

Some boys, who stood watching above by the fence,
Fell back in surprised and in speechless suspense
When his claws gripped the rail where he came to a stop,
And blazing, wild eyes met their eyes at the top.

Brief moments he balanced on top of the rail,
Just looking around to determine his trail.
Past memories rose to help show him the way
And beckoned him towards them this warm,
winter day.

To get back in his jungle
to roam wild and free
Filled much of his mind,
just as much as could be.

So straightway he leaped
    to flee fast from the zoo,
And frightened some folks
    when he came in their view.

He raced for his freedom with all of his might.
He raced toward the woods that he held in his sight.
That tawny, fine form disappeared in those trees.
Zookeepers seemed shocked he escaped with such ease.

Vast rumors ran rampant as where he had strayed.
This wild, spotted feline had people afraid.
The "Great Hunt" began for this wild, escaped beast.
Each moment the reign of his terror increased.

Folks peeked around corners,
in bushes, and under.
All shadows could move, and
each noise made them wonder.

The whole countryside
became jumpy and scared
For he had not been found,
and he had not been snared.

Marines and the Red Cross
each mobilized too.
They combed all the places
surrounding the zoo.

"Lion dogs" led the hunt,
    and folks trailed with their pets
To help track the feline
    that caused all the threats.

By air, helicopters and planes
joined the search.
For three days they scanned
from their lofty sky perch.

Civil Air and police rallied...
even the press
Got in on the hunt,
but with little success.

His tracks in some mud
by a pond folks discovered;
A farm where some cattle
stampeded they covered.

One section of brush grown
so thick needed burned,
But the leopard's location
remained to be learned.

Some meat that was soaked in a sleep remedy
Was placed by his cage for the leopard to see.
When his hunger once brought his return to the zoo,
They'd be ready and poised for the cat rendezvous.

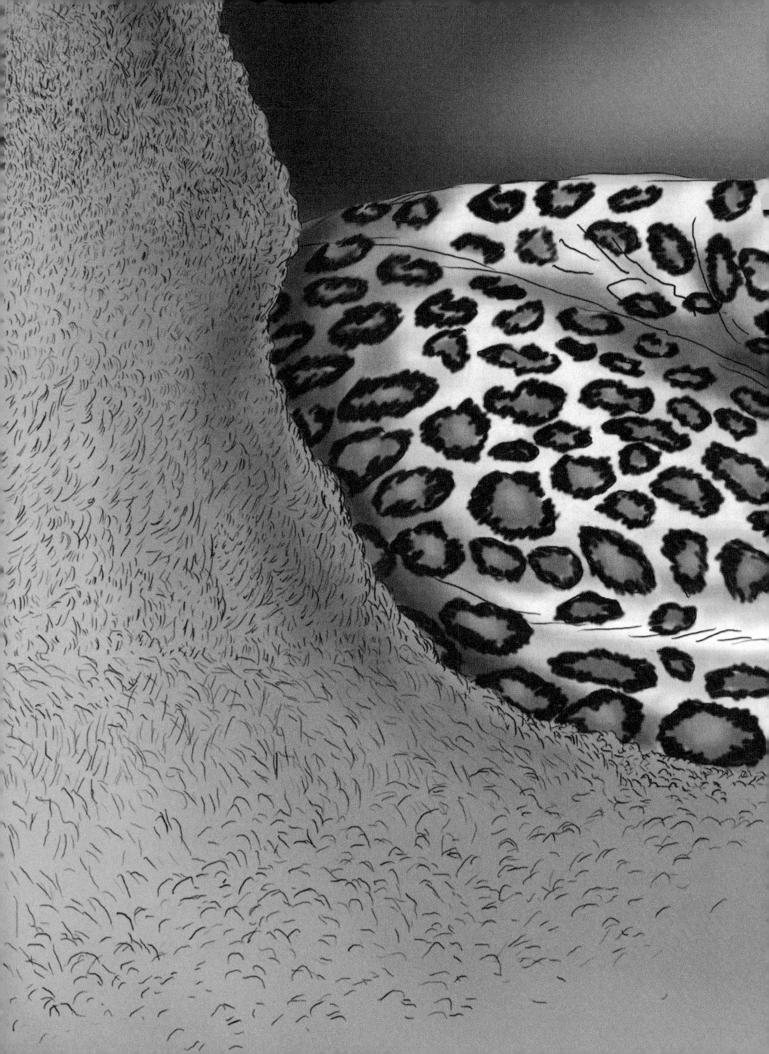

Under cover of darkness when hunger grew great,
The leopard returned for the meat, which he ate.
So groggy he grew that he hardly could creep
Where they found him curled up in his tunnel asleep.

Once he returned, the press
gave him a name,
Known simply as "Leapy",
to honor his fame.

With the "Great Hunt" now over
with all of its noise,
Store merchants sold t-shirts
and stuffed leopard toys!

Zookeepers made "Leapy" a room with a view
After once he returned to the OKC Zoo.
There from his new quarters, folks watched him with ease,
And through its glass wall, he could still see his trees.

listen|imagine|view|experience

AUDIO BOOK DOWNLOAD INCLUDED WITH THIS BOOK!

In your hands you hold a complete digital entertainment package. In addition to the paper version, you receive a free download of the audio version of this book. Simply use the code listed below when visiting our website. Once downloaded to your computer, you can listen to the book through your computer's speakers, burn it to an audio CD or save the file to your portable music device (such as Apple's popular iPod) and listen on the go!

How to get your free audio book digital download:

1. Visit www.tatepublishing.com and click on the elLIVE logo on the home page.
2. Enter the following coupon code:

   baaa-7fc4-e6c9-e68a-9631-6ab3-d3d0-ab23
3. Download the audio book from your elLIVE digital locker and begin enjoying your new digital entertainment package today!

CPSIA information can be obtained
at www.ICGtesting.com
Printed in the USA
LVOW05s2001300616

494820LV00006B/11/P